YOUR VOICE, GOD'S WORD
Reading the Bible in Church

YOUR VOICE, GOD'S WORD
Reading the Bible in Church

by

William Sydnor

MOREHOUSE-BARLOW
Wilton, Connecticut

Morehouse-Barlow Co., Inc.
78 Danbury Road
Wilton, Connecticut 06897

Library of Congress Cataloging-in-Publication Data

Sydnor, William.
  Your voice, God's word.

1. Lay readers.   I. Title.
BV677.S93   1988   264   88-9374
ISBN: 0-8192-1438-8

Printed in the United States of America
by
BSC LITHO
Harrisburg, PA

Dedication

To the readers who serve at the Sunday Eucharist in the Bethlehem Chapel of the Washington Cathedral every week. Their dedication is awesome and their performance is hard to match. They contribute more to the quality of worship than they realize.

Table of Contents

Preface ix

1. Then and Now 1

2. Who, Me? 7

3. The Mechanics of Your Job 11

4. Getting Ready 17

5. Teaching in Corporate Worship 23

6. Be Intelligible—Part I 27

7. Be Intelligible—Part II 31

8. The Hearing Event 39

9. Upon Hearing the Word of God 45

10. Look at the Whole Picture 49

    Appendix A 53

    Appendix B 55

Preface

The person who reads Scripture in a church service has a significant influence on the quality and meaning of the whole service and, possibly, on the lives of participants in that service. I am certain that most readers are not aware of the full gravity of their role in worship. Many ministers and priests also fail to appreciate the far-reaching effect of the performance of their lay Scripture readers.

This little monograph attempts to make that significance clear by dealing with the work of the reader on three levels. The basic level, of course, is elocution; the lector must master the fundamentals of his profession; all else depends on it. The second level is intelligibility. Worshipers must understand what they are hearing, if they are to learn from it. Hearing the Scripture read is the age-old way in which people learn the Bible's story. The third level is that of engendering faith. This last is too often overlooked.

This adds up to a very high opinion of the significance and importance of the reader's role. In the course of spelling it out, there are repeated references to the pastor under whom the reader serves. Clergy should, therefore, read what is contained here. Then they will understand why their conscientious readers who have read this book have, by the grace of God, caught a vision and are holding their heads a little higher. They will also be aware of the kind of support their lectors expect from them.

I am indebted to a host of readers for what they have taught me through the years about dedication, persistence,

devotion, teamwork, and a number of other things. I wish
I could name them all and thank them all. I thank God
that through the years they have crossed my path.

William Sydnor

February 24, 1988

Chapter 1

Then and Now

Once upon a time a Jewish synagogue named Beth Alpha was built a few miles south of where the Jordan River leaves the Sea of Galilee. The ruins show that the seating in that synagogue was in the round—a large oval, and there was a wide walkway behind the seats all around the room, which is said to have been the area used for study, perhaps the synagogue school. The open mosaic floor still exists, amazingly well preserved. It is in three parts showing the synagogue Holy of Holies, the Zodiac with figures for the four seasons, and Abraham about to sacrifice Isaac on the mountain. The date of this ruin is about 580 A.D. Scholars think that the floor plan of this ancient synagogue is similar to that of the synagogues of Jesus' day.

Having such a building floor plan in mind, consider Luke's account of Jesus' experience.

[Jesus] came to Nazareth, where he had been brought up; and he went to the synagogue, as was his custom, on the sabbath day. And he stood up to read [notice he did not come forward]; and there was given to him the book of the prophet Isaiah. He opened the book and found the place where it was written,
"The Spirit of the Lord is upon me, because he has anointed me to preach good news to the poor. He has sent me to proclaim release to the captives and recovering of sight to the blind, to set at liberty those

1

who are oppressed, to proclaim the acceptable year
of the Lord."
And he closed the book [it was actually a scroll], and
gave it back to the attendant, and sat down; and the
eyes of all in the synagogue were fixed on him. [He had
not moved from his place and yet all present could
easily see him.] And he began to say to them, "Today
this scripture has been fulfilled in your hearing."
(Lk. 4:16–21)

Jesus was an unordained layperson, reading the
Scripture in a service of corporate worship. In the
gatherings of Christian believers following Jesus' death
and resurrection, this practice was naturally continued.
And in time, the reader, naturally became the custodian
of the Christian writings which he was to read in worship.
Before a generation had passed, those scrolls included the
letters of Paul and other letters, Hebrews, for instance.
Not long after Paul's death (about 64 A.D.) the Gospels
began to appear. Mark around 70 A.D., Luke, Matthew,
and Acts between 80 and 90 A.D., and John around the
turn of the century. All these were added to the box of
scrolls of which the reader was the custodian.

It was not long, however, before the role of the reader
took on new seriousness. At the time of the Diocletian
persecution in 303 A.D., Scripture readers died because
they would not reveal the hiding place of their box of
precious Christian scrolls.[1] Those men and women
protected the sacred writings with their lives. The reader
of God's word in worship had become one of great
importance in the life of the Church, and it was a role

[1]Dom Gregory Dix, *The Shape of the Liturgy,* New York: Seabury
Press, 1983, pp. 24–26.

held by laypersons. Unfortunately, this was shortly to begin to undergo a change.

In Alexandria, Egypt, there appeared on the scene a spell-binding preacher named Arius. The gist of his message was that Jesus of Nazareth was a very unusual person, who should be followed and emulated, but he was not the Son of God. This contradicted the usual profession of faith which was part of the rite of baptism of every Christian. That Apostles' Creed stated:

> I believe in God, the Father almighty,
>   creator of heaven and earth.
> I believe in Jesus Christ, his only Son,
>   our Lord.
> He was conceived by the power of the
>   Holy Spirit
>   and born of the Virgin Mary.

Here was a sharp difference. Was Jesus Christ only a human being, or was he also the Son of God? Christians began to argue and question.

The Roman Empire had spread around the Mediterranean basin and beyond—different peoples, cultures, nations, all under the authority of Emperor Constantine of Rome. The emperor decided that the obvious unifying factor within his empire was the Christian Church; it was everywhere. If he could get the Christians to agree among themselves and stop squabbling about the nature of Jesus Christ, he would have brought about the unity he desired. With this idea in mind, he called a meeting of Christian leaders at his summer palace at Nicea in 325 A.D. He formally opened the meeting and then commanded those church leaders (bishops, most of them) to come to an agreement as to what they believed about Jesus Christ.

The outcome of that first General Church Council was the Nicene Creed, which emphatically stressed the divinity of Jesus Christ while in no way diminishing belief in his humanity:

> We believe in one Lord, Jesus Christ,
>   the only Son of God,
> eternally begotten of the Father,
> God from God, Light from Light,
> true God from true God,
> begotten, not made,
> of one Being with the Father. . . .
> he became incarnate from the Virgin Mary,
>   and was made man. . . .

It was probably because of the emphasis on the Lord's divinity that gradually in the centuries that followed worship accented holiness, an awesome separateness. It was something to be done only by set-apart, ordained ministers. This awesomeness in the presence of God gradually created a barrier between laypersons and ordained clergy. The reader's status became an office which was considered a minor order of clergy. Lay participation was boxed out. Laypersons became spectators. In the Middle Ages, the celebration of the eucharist became less and less a communal activity and an almost private act of the priest.

The reformation in the sixteenth century began to change this. Martin Luther talked of the "priesthood of all believers." *The Book of Common Prayer* of the Church of England put the liturgy in the hands of the people and expected them to begin taking a responsible part in every act of corporate worship. But it was not until the twentieth century that change began to come about which brought laypersons' participation in corporate worship back to what it had once been in the first century.

In the 1930s, forward-looking clergy of all denominations were beginning to be involved in liturgical renewal. Two tangible results of that movement were the Vatican II document, *Constitution On the Sacred Liturgy,* in 1964 and *The Book of Common Prayer* revision in 1979. In each case a layperson is intended to be the reader of the one or two passages of Scripture which occur before the Gospel. In the Episcopal Church, this prerogative includes the reading of Scripture in every service of corporate worship.

That is where we are today.

Chapter 2

Who, Me?

It is easy to be a back pew participant in corporate worship. Then one day the minister or priest asks, "Wouldn't you like to be a lay reader?" "Who, me?" Surely he or she has mistaken me for someone else. ME leave the security of my back pew and stand up front, one of the leaders in the worship of God's people!

What is involved?

The first thing which is involved is commitment. Am I willing to make this assignment a top priority? Am I going to take it seriously and work at it? Am I prepared to learn, and will I be anxious to grow in the job? Do I think of it as an honor or a chore? Will I give it my best shot *every time?* These are the kinds of questions one must ask himself/herself.

The next consideration is preparation. This starts with one's attitude of mind. What is to be my special part in the drama of corporate worship? When I have become aware of the contribution my reading is intended to make to that drama, I approach it under the banners of prayer, preparation, and practice.

Prayer: I am to be the voice which proclaims God's Word, so I begin on my knees, seeking to know how to serve him faithfully and well.

Preparation: This includes all the background information I need to know in order to read my assignment properly.

Practice: This involves the hard work of getting my assignment well in hand.

All of these will be dealt with in detail in what follows.

In the process of preparation and execution, one experiences a lot of butterflies in the stomach. This is not necessarily crippling stage fright. There is a healthy nervousness which old "pros" consider an asset. Bishop R.E.L. Strider of West Virginia was one of the outstanding preachers of the Episcopal Church a generation or so ago. He said he was always nervous when he stepped into the pulpit. Then he added, "But would you rather be a race horse or a milch cow?" And Chris Evert, the professional women's tennis player, who had just won her first round match in her seventeenth U.S. Open Tennis Tournament, was asked if she had been nervous. She replied, "Of course. The day I stop getting nervous is the day I quit tennis."

However, some of us find that we dread getting on our feet in front of a crowd. The experience brings on a frozen helplessness. (If this does not apply to you, skip the rest of this chapter and go on to the next.) "What can I do? I really want to be a lay reader. Can I conquer my stage fright?" You may have to grow out of it, like adolescence. There are, however, numerous quick-fix remedies just as there are for hiccups. Some of them will help some people. A drama department professor at West Virginia University named Mrs. Fear (that was really her name) used to advise students consciously to keep their knees from shaking and consciously to make their voices calm and reassuring. "It will calm you," she said. Maybe in your case she is right. However, continual practice aloud at home and before audiences is probably the best way to overcome stage fright.

Stage fright is a form of self-consciousness. Think about what you are up there to do. People did not come to the church to look at you. They came to hear God's Word. They are not likely to remember you unless you insist on calling attention to yourself by your fumbling performance, but hopefully they will remember what you read. You are a voice, an instrument in the service of God. No one is interested in a painter's instruments, his brushes, it is the picture he produces which they remember and treasure. Think yourself out of the scene. Concentrate on the message from God's Word you are trying to proclaim.

That does not work? Every time you even think of standing up before those people your knees feel weak and your palms get damp? That's all right. Maybe it is God's way of telling you that reading in public is not something you are intended to do. "Thank you, no," she said, "That is not my bag." She became an usher and is a very faithful one. The Lord accepts us as we are and uses our different abilities in different ways.

Chapter 3

The Mechanics of Your Job

Speaking to an assembly is different from talking with several individuals in your living room. In order to be intelligible to that fellow in the back row, you must speak more slowly and more distinctly. I can toss ping-pong balls to you one after another faster than you can catch them. In the same way, I can toss you words, one after another, faster than you can absorb them; the greater the distance the slower I have to speak in order to be understood. To some extent children are aware of this. Big sister comes out on the doorstep and shouts to her kid brother halfway down the block, "MOTH . . . ERR . . . SEZ . . . COME . . . HOME . . . RIGHT . . . NOW!" That is a bit exaggerated, but you get the idea. Speak more slowly than is normal and ennunciate clearly, as though you were seeking to be helpful to someone who reads lips.

Irvin Berlin once said of Ethel Merman, "Don't ever give her bad lyrics. The people in the back row are sure to hear every word of them." Ethel Merman knew how to pronounce words and how to project her voice. These were fundamental to everything she did on the stage, and they are fundamental for every lector.

Here are some suggestions which will help the novice at public reading become more proficient:

The tendency to race pell-mell through the reading is a common fault of inexperienced readers. To counter this, consciously read, as we said earlier, with a calm voice and measured tempo. It will do much toward dissipating that very natural nervousness.

Also be aware of dropping your voice at the end of a sentence, as a result of which the hearers fail to get the last word. Approach a period like an airplane approaches a landing strip, gradually come down. But do not forget that guy in the back row. Come down, but don't drop off his radar screen.

The fledgling reader is likely to find this difficult to do because he runs out of breath. This happens because the reader is using the shallow breathing of ordinary speech. Lungs have a great capacity for air, which the speaker must learn to use. Practice filling your lungs from the bottom.

I talked with a voice expert about what readers might do to develop a larger lung supply of breath. I hope this is an accurate account (translation?) of what he told me. First you have to know that the diaphragm is a petition separating the cavity containing the lungs from the lower cavity, the abdomen. In order to fill the lower parts of the lungs, the diaphragm has to relax, not pressing upward. Observe the breathing of a tiny baby. His stomach expands as he inhales. The muscles which we train to hold in our stomachs, let go; the stomach sags, the diaphragm relaxes and ceases to press against and cramp the lungs. Professional singers have learned this infant technique. They relax a host of muscles in the abdomen so that there is no upward pressure, then they can fill their lungs to capacity.

Now here is what I suggest: Stand up straight. Relax your abdomen; let your stomach go. Feel it pressing against your belt as you slowly inhale. Fill your lungs all the way up, then exhale gradually, steadily, and taking as long as you can. Now, when you have gotten a handle on this technique, take your favorite biblical passage and read as much as you can with your supply of breath. Mark the spot. Try again; hopefully this time you will be able to read a little further. Repeat this routine five or six times every few days, and you are likely to experience greater breath control when you read in church.

One of the places where proper breathing is indispensable is in relation to punctuation. In the text, punctuation marks are intended to help make the material intelligible. Your hearers gather the same assistance to intelligibility from your inflections and pauses. Perhaps the best way to master this art is to listen to a tape recording of your reading. Listen with the book closed. Does your rendition give the true sense of the text? In the Christmas story, for instance, ignored punctuation can have the shepherds coming to Bethlehem and finding Mary and Joseph and the babe all lying in the manger together. There is a comma after Joseph. Your voice has to tell us that; and the same with all other punctuation. Only practice with a tape recorder will tell you whether you are verbally punctuating the passage properly, and at the same time being true to the flow of words and phrases.

Quotation marks tell us, of course, that someone is speaking directly. Sometimes this is written into the text, sometimes it is not. Your hearers need to know who is talking. You may be able to make the change in speakers evident by a pause, but most of us are not skilled enough to accomplish this. So when the speaker is not indicated in the text, hearers are likely to find the passage confusing, if the reader does not help them. This will often be true in reading the Old Testament prophets. Jeremiah 3:21–23 is a case in point:

A voice on the bare heights is heard,
  the weeping and pleading of Israel's sons,
because they have perverted their way,
    they have forgotten the Lord their God.
[*The Lord said to them,*]
"Return, O faithless sons,
    I will heal your faithlessness."
[*And the people of Israel replied,*]
"Behold, we come to thee;
    for thou art the Lord our God.
Truly the hills are a delusion,
    the orgies on the mountains.
Truly in the Lord our God
    is the salvation of Israel."

When more than one person speaks in the course of your assigned passage, there is the temptation to become dramatic. But yours is not a stage performance; you do not want to call attention to yourself. Rather seek to convey the differences—prophet and God, father and son, Jesus and leper—by what you are thinking, dramatically but much underplayed.

Mastering the skills of elocution: proper breathing; the proper use of pauses for emphasis and intelligibility; maintaining the flow of words and phrases; pleasing diction; and all the rest, is a demanding discipline. It requires continual practice until those skills become second nature, like the basketball player's ability to dribble the ball. This is not something one can learn from a book. No one ever learned to swim by reading a book. You have to get in the water, and you need a coach if you expect to be an excellent swimmer. The lector should approach the skills of elocution with the same seriousness.

The person who has the most experience in speaking

in the church building in which you will be reading is your minister. He or she has both the training and the experience of making the human voice distinctly heard in that particular auditorium. He/she hears you perform and knows what you are doing right and what you are doing wrong. He/she is the one who is best qualified to encourage you, to analyze mistakes, to make constructive criticism. Your minister is your on-the-spot coach, or can put you in touch with a trained person who can assist you.

Friends have warned that a reader cannot count on his minister to be a dependable voice coach or even to think the matter is very important. Some ministers are horrible public readers and do not consider the art of public speaking one to cultivate. Happily this is not a widespread malaise. But if it is your unfortunate situation, take the initiative. Find your own coach—a high school drama teacher, someone at the local college, a voice teacher. Remember, in worship we are offering our best to God. You cannot offer God your best if you do not know how to produce it.

This is no job for a sweet friend who will give you false compliments. Honest criticism usually deflates, but when it is coupled with constructive advice the serious reader can through persistence hone his/her skills. Ethel Merman was not heard in the back row the first few times she tried.

Your minister or priest *should* take the initiative in this, for it is unquestionably his/her responsibility. The services for the congregation should be the best that the clergy-lay team can produce. You who read the Scripture have a major role to play in the drama of Sunday worship, as is made clear in subsequent chapters. Your minister and you should aspire to have your readings done to the very best of your ability. This will not happen without practice and coaching. As actor Sammy Davis, Jr., has said, "It is hard to amount to much unless you learn the basics."

After you are well on the road to mastering the mechanics of your job, you are *ready to begin* to become a good reader. Now you must find the answer to the question, "What am I doing when I read Scripture in public worship?" A church service is not a haphazard collection of pious activities—hymns, prayers, readings, sermon. It is, as we have said above, a drama in which people come into the presence of God. What role do you, the reader of Scripture, play in that drama? This we shall try to answer so that you may experience the humbling excitement of your commission.

Chapter 4

Getting Ready

You are a new Scripture reader and have received your assignment well in advance, at least a week ahead. How shall you prepare?

There are, of course, numerous ways to go about it. Here are a few. One gifted reader says he always reads the passage in several versions, in order to get the "feel" of it. Some read it over every day during the week before in order to become "at home" with it. One person makes his assigned passage part of his daily devotions during that preceding week. Still another says she reads several chapters, sometimes even the whole book of which her assigned reading is a part. "I want to know the context of my assignment," she said. Ultimately, the best preparation is to read it aloud standing in front of a mirror, briefly looking up occasionally. A concert singer says that she goes over her assigned reading as often and as carefully as she does the music she is going to sing on stage. On a recent Sunday, a person who had been complimented on the excellent way in which she had read the Scripture that morning responded with a note of surprise, "Y'know, I found I was almost reciting it"—evidence of her thorough preparation. Other seasoned readers have said the same thing. Of course, be certain you are rehearsing with the same version of the Bible as that from which you will be reading in church.

When the day comes, get to church early. Double

check the physical setup. Find your place in the lectern
Bible, know where your reading starts on the page. Is the
lighting normal? A last minute burned out bulb in the
chancel can put the reader at a disadvantage. Are there
any unusual decorations which impede your route to the
lectern? Check the public address system. Is it turned on
and at proper volume? Check everything, everytime. You
want to avoid any surprises which will distract you when
the time comes and will curtail your effectiveness.

A major getting-there-early responsibility is to report
to your minister or priest in person, whether he requires
it or not. It is a matter of simple courtesy to let him or
her know that you as a member of his team for that service
are on hand. Some clergy not only have the reader report
in before the service, they also have them present for the
before-service prayer which he or she has with the
members of the worship team for that service.

Sit near the front on the aisle. Getting up should not
be a hassle. You should be well on your way to the lectern
by the time the congregation is comfortably settled after
sitting down following what immediately preceded the
reading.

One's attire is also important. Nothing about one's
dress or hair style should call special attention to you as
a person. One's attire should be conservative and befitting
the dignity of the occasion. Neither high style nor flam-
boyant colors are appropriate. (This is not just addressed
to women. Some men's neckties could be used to flag a
train at midnight.) At the other extreme, the casual attire
of an afternoon cookout is also out of place. Nothing
about the person who is getting ready to read God's Word
should distract hearers from giving that reading their full
attention.

As you move forward to read, you begin to set the stage for your contribution to the worship of the day. Think: **Something important is about to happen, God willing.** It is not that "*I* am going to read the Bible to you folks." This is not a public reading performance, such as an actor would do on a theater stage. The spotlight there is on the actor. In this instance, the spotlight (if there be one) is on the lectern, the Bible, God's Word. And you? You are the voice that will proclaim it.

Remember how the gospels introduce John the Baptist?

> ". . . The Jews [i.e., the authorities] sent priests and Levites from Jerusalem to ask John, 'Who are you?' " He could have basked in the light of his sudden, center-stage prominence and preened himself in studied humility before this official delegation, saying, "I am just a poor parson's son. My father, Zachariah of the division of Abijah, takes his regular turn serving in the Temple. If my humble words have attracted wide-spread attention, God be praised." No. John sought to put the spotlight on his God-given message, not himself: "I am the voice of one crying in the wilderness" (Jn. 1:19, 23).

At the 1986 Wimbledon Tennis Tournament, Chris Evert Lloyd talked with reporters about body language— what one's whole stance reveals about how one really feels: "When a player really thinks they can win, they start to strut around a little. When they don't really believe in themselves, you can see them hang their heads a little on big points. You have to learn to read it." After the day's matches one reporter picked on this body language theme. "The underdogs never really understood. They looked up and saw the strut, the look of confidence. The belief. And so they doubted—and lost.''[1] One's set of mind is a tremendous factor in accomplishing one's purpose.

Think of who you, the reader, are. You are going up to that lectern to be the voice that proclaims God's Word. You believe that something important is about to happen, and, by the grace of God, you are to be the agent in bringing it about. Think yourself out of the picture and think the voice of God in. You shed the tattered rags of self-consciousness and don the glorious apparel of a proclaiming voice in God's service.

In at least one great church in this country, the other members of the corps of lectors pray for the reader of the day as he or she moves toward the lectern. What marvelous support!

In addition, the ambiance of the setting supports the reader in his intended purpose. The building, the people, the music, the choir, and all the rest proclaim the occasion a propitious one. One important detail is the great Bible before which you stand. Should your situation be one in which you are to read from the Bible you bring forward with you, be certain it is a book of proper size and dignity. No paperback, no pocket-size volume.[2] Every detail points to or detracts from the importance of that which is about to take place. One must do everything possible not to hinder the miracle of revelation.

[1] *Washington Post,* 2 July 1987.
[2] Easily readable print is important. The lighting in church is not likely to be as strong as your desk lamp at home. Bible versions with larger than normal print are hard to find. World Bible Publishers, Iowa Falls, Iowa, has what it calls a Large Print Edition of the RSV which many have found satisfactory.

The person who comes forward to read looks like he or she knows something important is about to take place. Thomas Merton is not wide of the mark when he likens the Eucharist to a ballet. The poise of him who is about to read God's Word is not so much a studied stance, which can be mere play acting, rather it is an attitude of mind. Then let the body produce its own proper stance.

Now you are set to do a good job. As the popular song puts it, "Everything's going my way." Take a deep breath as you look out at the congregation, and let it out slowly. Single out someone in the back row and tell him what is about to happen. That is what your introductory comment is, about which we shall have more to say later (p. 35). Then make your official announcement: **A reading from the Book of Daniel.** Do not tell them what chapter and verse; you want them to listen, not look it up.

Deep down inside you are convinced that Roger Shattuck is right: oral interpretation "restores the freshness and urgence of older works."[3] Your aspiration is that by the grace of God this may be true now for your hearers.

[3]Roger Shattuck, *The Innocent Eye on Modern Literature and the Arts,* (New York: Farrar Straus Giroux, 1984), p. 321.

Chapter 5

Teaching in Corporate Worship

Corporate worship has several dimensions. Among them are mystery, drama, teaching, faith, and proclaiming the Word. Let us take a closer look at how teaching is done through the church service itself. The sermon is intentionally omitted in this discussion, because preaching in worship is a whole different subject which is outside the province of readers.

Early Christians gathered regularly to worship the God and Father of our Lord Jesus Christ and to hear over and over all that Jesus did and taught. The hearing of the Word was the principal way in which the story of redemption was passed on from generation to generation. There are no records of educational programs *per se.* Teaching was done in the context of worship.

Very early, the Lord's resurrection was celebrated regularly on the first day of the week and annually at the time of year when the Jews were observing the Passover. Gradually, commemoration of events leading up to the crucifixion-resurrection began. Probably an Easter vigil came first. Then gradually observance of Good Friday, Maundy Thursday, Palm Sunday, and the whole of Holy Week followed. Succeeding generations of church observance completed the pre-resurrection cycle with the forty days of Lent. In like manner the Easter season itself was also developing. Following the Lucan sequence of events, the observance of Ascension and Pentecost came into being.

A similar series of annual observances began to cluster around the Lord's nativity. It was observed annually on December 25th in the West and January 6th in the East. The Advent season of four weeks celebrated the Old Testament preparation for the coming of the Messiah. In time, the January 6th observance became the Epiphany, which along with succeeding weeks celebrated the fact that the newborn Jesus was the savior of the world, not just the long-awaited Jewish messiah.

So it is that the Christian year came into being, telling the story of redemption with calendar regularity. When this calendar schedule is set over against the Bible, we begin to see how complete this annual observance of Christian teaching is:

Advent	Old Testament
Christmas	Nativity
Epiphany, Lent and Holy Week, Easter	The rest of the gospel record
Ascension	The end of the gospels and Acts 1
Pentecost	Acts 2
Pentecost season	The rest of the New Testament

The creeds put this same biblical drama of salvation into a verbal affirmation.

Since the appointed Scripture for a given Sunday or feast day has been selected because of its appropriateness on that occasion, a great deal of unheralded teaching takes place. The Scripture read adds dimensions of meaning to the occasion or season in which it is heard. At the same time, the fact that people hear an Old Testament reading at Christmastime, for instance, helps them appreciate that reading more, since they now see in it a dimension of the meaning of the Christmas event. These are like two mirrors reflecting into each other. Because of the Scripture which is heard, the season takes on deeper meaning; and the season or feast day when the Scripture is read may give that Scripture a dimension it did not have before.

There is yet another teaching mirror present in every service—the theme running through the Scripture passages read in that service. In celebrating the Feast of the Epiphany, we hear the poetry of Second Isaiah (Is. 60:1, 3):

> Arise, shine; for your light has come, . . .
> And nations shall come to your light,
> and kings to the brightness of your rising.

The Magi saga has its commentary. Moreover, the significance of the Epiphany season has been spelled out.

So we see that there is a definite, well-ordered annual plan of teaching in worship which has ancient and history-tested roots. The Christian year attaches the biblical drama to the calendar. The appointed Scriptures elaborate in weekly installments on the details of God's relation to humankind. In the services, there is this built-in interaction between the theme of the service, the seasonal emphasis, and the biblical readings. This was the principal teaching program of the Church for some eighteen hundred years. The printing press had to be invented before the Sunday school and Bible study groups and the family Bible could come on the scene.

Today corporate worship continues to be the primary teaching media of the Church. The Bible's story is proclaimed week by week somewhat like a novel which appears chapter by chapter in serial fashion in a weekly magazine. In the course of every twelve months, worshipers hear the whole drama of redemption proclaimed.

You, the reader, are one of the agents in this process of proclamation and that is no slight responsibility.

When the conscientious lector realizes that the reading of Scripture is the centerpiece in the Church's teaching ministry, a host of questions come to mind.

*How is reading in a church service any different from reading in any other public gathering?

*If there is a difference, how is one to convey that fact to the assembled hearers?

*Since teaching is a large component of the role of reading the Scripture, what should one do to help make the material he or she reads intelligible?

*Recognizing that corporate worship has several dimensions, what role does the reading of Scripture in worship play in areas other than teaching?

These are some of the questions we now seek to answer.

Chapter 6

Be Intelligible—Part I

A part of the secret of the effective reading of Scripture in worship is that the passage must make sense to you, the reader, and it must make sense to your hearers. This is so fundamental and obvious that we nod, "Of course, of course," and brush it aside as we go on to some other consideration. But wait: not so fast.

There are two fundamentals of intelligible Bible reading which I consider so basic and are so widely ignored that they should be called "laws." They are laws to me. You might call them "Sydnor's Laws."

The first law is this: *The reading must make sense to you, if it is to make sense to your hearers.* So research your assigned reading. Do not assume that the meaning will be clear to the congregation. What Paul says about speaking in tongues applies here: Unless you are making sense, "you might just as well be addressing an empty room" (J.B. Phillips, 1 Cor. 14:9).

Get familiar with your assignment in context. A study Bible or a one-volume commentary or some succinct analysis of the appointed lections will help you appreciate the nest in which your assigned egg rests.[1]

The story is told of a refugee from Nazi Germany who in the 1930s began his studies at Cincinnati's Hebrew

---

[1]Your parish library may have a copy of my *Sunday's Scriptures* (Wilton, CT: Morehouse-Barlow Co., Inc.), which is now out of print.

Union College. One day he saw a startling newspaper headline, "REDS MURDER CARDINALS." "Oui, Oui, Oui!" he thought, "A revolution in Italy." Of course, everyone else in Cincinnati knew that the Cincinnati Reds had defeated the St. Louis Cardinals in baseball. "But how was I to know?" he protested. "I didn't have the context." Then he added, "Will not an archeologist a thousand years hence come across this item and conclude that the communists occupied Italy and decimated the Vatican?"

One must know the context if the passage is to be intelligible, and also if one is to know how to read it. Here is an example of how important this is. Consider these beautiful words from Hosea 6:1-2:

> Come, let us return to the Lord;
> for he has torn, that he may heal us;
> for he has stricken, and he will bind us up.
> After two days he will revive us;
> on the third day he will raise us up,
> that we may live before him.

Beautiful! Uplifting! Here is penitence which challenges and inspires us. But wait, look carefully at the context (5:15-6:5). When we read these words in their proper setting, we discover that our initial impression that they are genuine and sincere is misleading. They are a complacent and facile expression of penitence. They express the shallowness of the popular religious attitude which the prophet was addressing and which borders on cynicism. Like Voltaire, the people were saying, "God will forgive; that's his business." "There is no sense of awe before God, no sense of the loss of an intimate relationship which can only be gradually restored, no searching sense of guilt before divine law and the need for spiritual cleansing."[2]

Knowing the context is very important. Apart from an appreciation of the context of the passage, the reading is likely to be a misreading.

Experienced readers, as we said earlier, often read their assignment in several different translations in order, as one of them put it, "to get the feel of it." It is likely that one translation of your assignment will appeal to you more than the others. In some churches, the lector may read from his own Bible rather than using the one on the lectern. Should you have this liberty, be certain to have permission from the preacher of the service to use the version you prefer. Here is why this is so important: On one occasion the Old Testament reading was from Daniel 7, the description of who the heavenly Son of Man is. Since Jesus characteristically used Son of Man in referring to himself, the preacher saw this as an opportunity to explain the term and the use of it. The reader, however, thinking of his assigned task as an isolated event, decided to read from the New English Bible in which there is no mention of a Son of Man (as there is in the Revised Standard Version), but instead there is the phrase "one like a man coming on the clouds of heaven." Consequently, the preacher was put in the position of explaining away the Scripture reading.

The reader is not a solo performer; the preacher and the reader of the Word have complementary roles. The reading without the sermon runs the danger of losing its relevance, its application to life, and the sermon that pays no attention to the reading runs the danger of being

[2]*The Interpreter's Bible* (Nashville, Abingdon Press, 1956) 6:624.

one person's subjective reflections on the divine-human situation.

Good reading in church, becoming at home with one's assignment, learning how to have it make sense to you, is hard work. It takes time and determination, but it is all worth it. In the Old Testament, there are many awesome references to "the glory of the Lord." One of them reads, "the glory of the Lord filled the house of God" (2 Chr. 5:14). Now and then it happens even today, and your reading may be such as occasion. Do your best to be the voice of God's Word, and no telling what may happen. Because the reading now makes sense to you, it may now make glorious sense to your hearers.

So you see why Sydnor's first law of intelligibility is important. *The reading must make sense to you if it is to make sense to your hearers.*

Chapter 7

Be Intelligible—Part II

The second law of intelligibility is this: *Put yourself in your hearers' place. Tell them what they need to know in order to find the passage intelligible.*

This is one of the oldest liturgical practices in the Judeo-Christian tradition. In the fifth century B.C., when the Israelites had returned to newly rebuilt Jerusalem from Babylonian captivity, there was a great service of rededication. In the course of it, Ezra, the Levite, and his colleagues brought "the book of the law of Moses which the Lord had given to Israel," and the Levites "read from the book, from the law of God, clearly; and they gave the sense, so that the people understood the reading" (Neh. 8:1, 8).

In what way must we "give the sense, so that the people understand the reading?"

The reading is from the Bible, which is a diverse library of books written during the course of at least a dozen centuries by a large number of authors. The appointed readings on a given Sunday have been carefully selected from somewhere in the middle of some of the Bible's sixty-six books. Some passages are familiar to a reasonable number of the assembled worshipers. Some are familiar only to those whose bedside companion is a worn Bible. There is the possibility that a number of people may, by the grace of God, be really hearing the day's reading with new ears—if not for the first time, it may be the first intelligent time, the first time the reading has "spoken" to them. So for some present, the hearing of the Word on this day can be a signal occasion, memorable and significant.

There are two procedures which are necessary in order to help bring this about. They are (1) lead-ins and (2) introductory comments. Here is what I mean.

Lead-ins

The reader's assigned passage is a paragraph or two, as we said, in the middle of one of the Bible's many books. It is part of a story, a letter, a poem, or whatever. The opening sentence of that passage is not likely to be an opening sentence at all; it is intimately linked to that which went before. Something has to be done to unhitch it from what immediately precedes it so that there is an intelligible opening sentence.

Here are some obvious changes which need to be made for the sake of intelligence. Nouns have to replace pronouns. "He said to him, 'Follow me' . . ." has to become "Jesus said to Levi, 'Follow me.' . . ." Connecting conjunctions must be omitted. "And on the first day of the week. . . ." The reading is only about what happened on the first day of the week; omit the "And." Adverbs also can have a backward look. "Then," "now," "after this" all imply that hearers are aware of what preceded the passage at hand.

A good practice is to read the opening sentence and then think about it as though you were a thoughtful member of the congregation. Is there some suggestion here that I should know what has gone before? "That something," the thoughtful hearer muses, "may have significance for appreciation of this present passage. I should have been told what it is." You do not want your thoughtful hearers wasting their attention in a guessing game about what went before and therefore failing to give their full attention to the reading at hand. The lead-in, then, is whatever revision or addition to the opening sentence has to be made in order that hearers may savor the passage at hand with no teasing aftertaste because of some previous detail they cannot identify.

A few years back, there was a musical on the Broadway stage called *Jumpers.* When the curtain went up for the first time, the audience saw a professor's office on some college campus. His secretary was already at her desk. The professor enters, takes off his overcoat and hat, starts pacing, head down, hands behing him. Dictation is about to begin; the secretary's pencil is at the ready. He clears his throat and begins, "Secondly." Of course, the audience laughed; they were supposed to.

Now consider another drama: a church service. The lector approaches the lectern; he is going to read the Word of God. The congregation sits, and everyone's eyes are on the reader. He begins, "They said, 'This is a hard saying. . . .' " Nobody laughs. It is not supposed to be funny, but it is—or rather, pathetic. Any attentive, thinking person would, of course, ask himself, "Who's talking to whom, and what was the hard saying?" If the appointed reading is John 6:60–69, which begins in this fashion, the reader owes it to his hearers to pick up on an earlier verse as an intelligent lead-in. Here it is:

> Many of Jesus' disciples heard him say, "As the living Father sent me, and I live because of the Father, so he who eats me will live because of me." They said, "This is a hard saying" (Jn. 6:57, 60).

In addition to unhooking the appointed reading from what has gone before, hearers, of course, need to be told who is speaking when the opening sentence is in quotation marks, as was pointed out earlier (p. 13). Sometimes a person or a place mentioned in that opening sentence also needs to be identified.

Here are some lead-in examples, enough to give you a feel for what is necessary so that the opening sentence will not be a distracting red herring.

**Reading—1 Kg. 19:9–18, opening sentence: "And there he came to a cave, and lodged there; and behold, the word of the Lord came to him . . ."

Lead-in: "On Horeb, the mount of God, Elijah came to a cave and lodged there; and behold . . ."

**Reading—Hos. 2:14–23, opening sentence: " 'Therefore, behold, I will allure her, and bring her into the wilderness, and speak tenderly to her.' " The text is in quotation marks: identify the speaker. It is also necessary to make clear who Israel is in relation to the speaker.

Lead-in: "Thus says the Lord, 'I will allure [Israel, my unfaithful bride,] and bring her into the wilderness, and speak tenderly to her.' "

**Reading— Neh. 9:16–20, opening sentence: " 'But they and our fathers acted presumptuously and stiffened their necks and did not obey thy commandments.' " Another direct quotation. Neh. 9:6 is where this prayer begins.

Lead-in: "Ezra prayed, 'O Lord God, our fathers acted presumptuously and stiffened their necks . . .' "

**Reading—Mk. 4:35–41, opening sentence: "On that day, when evening had come, he said to them, 'Let us go . . .' " Do hearers wonder what happened "On that day?" Tell them.

Lead-in: "After a day of teaching, when evening had come, Jesus said to his disciples, 'Let us go . . .' "

**Reading—Lk. 9:28-36, opening sentence: "Now about eight days after these sayings he took with him Peter and James and John and went . . ."

Lead-in: "Now about eight days after Peter had first voiced the disciples growing conviction that Jesus was the Christ, Jesus took Peter and James and John . . ."

Quite obviously, lead-ins play a very important part in making the appointed scripture reading intelligible to a congregation of listeners. *But it is imperative that the reader get the approval of her/his minister or priest before using the proposed lead-in sentence in the service.*

Just as a lead-in is important for an intelligent appreciation of the lections read in worship, so also is an introductory comment before the reading.

Introductory Comment

Some years back, a disc jockey introduced a popular song on the air with this comment, "Now about this next: actually the words don't make much sense, mostly hodge-podge. But it's pretty. Listen to it." (Song, "Clear Day," Mar. 1966). So his hearers were wisely advised to appreciate a pretty melody and not be thrown off by the stupid words.

Common sense tells us that hearers need some orientation as to what they are about to hear if they are to listen intelligibly. They need to be clued in, get their bearings. That is the only way hearers are likely to appreciate the reading. But to prepare the right kind of introductory comment is not easy.

Charles Morgan has written that "the function of an artist [painter] is to enable vision in others. . . . Not to tell them what their vision should be. . . . the duty is not to impose his vision upon men but to open their eyes."[1] The person who reads scripture in corporate worship has a similar responsibility. He is an enabler of another's vision of divine truth. What he says in introducing the reading should not impose his vision upon his hearers. Remember, he is commissioned to help his hearers hear the passage, then he stands aside in order that the Lord's promise may come true: "The Holy Spirit, whom the Father will send in my name, he will teach you all things" (Jn. 14:26). There is no guarantee that this will happen, but do not lock out the possibility for such an occurrence.

The reader's temptation is to go beyond his commission and usurp the role of the Spirit of truth. The reader goes beyond his province when he tells his hearers what they ought to think about that which they are about to hear or presumes to tell them what it means. This is the inviting role of a propagandist. Everyone is tempted to tell others what they ought to think and believe, and how they ought to react to the word they are about to hear. It takes great discipline to resist the temptation to be preachy.

The introductory comment should in no respect be an extra sermon. Exposition belongs to the preacher. The introductory comment should be a brief, carefully worded statement. It should not upstage the reading to follow. It is the gangplank to get people aboard; it should not presume to be the ship of salvation. It is intended to give hearers a handle so that they can pick up the reading and examine it for themselves.

Put yourself in your hearers' place. What do they need

---

[1]Quoted by Mary MacDermott Shideler, *In Search of the Spirit,* (N.Y.: Ballantine Books, 1985), p. 200.

to know in order to appreciate what they are about to hear? Is the reading part of a sermon or a bit of history? Do they need to know the conflict being addressed or the tension being reacted to? Do they need to be aware of the larger context of which this reading is the climax, or the bias of the author, or the historical setting? These are some of the kinds of questions one must think about in deciding what needs to be said. Then strive to say it in about two sentences. This is not an easy assignment, obviously.

The introduction should be carefully written out and *given as written, word for word.* The composed introduction needs to be very clear and of studied brevity. The person who ad-libs and gives the gist of the prepared introduction invariably talks too long, spoiling the effectiveness of the introduction and sometimes even making the reading which follows seem ridiculously short.

Ideally the minister in charge of the service composes the introductory comment. He/she has the biblical background and is thinking about the service in its entirety. There are also printed introductions on the market which can be purchased.[2] If, however, the introduction is composed by the reader, *it should certainly be cleared with the minister before it is used.* One caution: regardless of who composes it, the reader should not say anything he or she does not fully understand.

I am convinced that if there is no well-informed introductory comment, the Word of God heard through the distorting earphones of ignorance may completely violate the meaning of the passage from Holy Writ. Could the devil have a more effective confederate?

---

[2] *Illuminations,* 90 Harrison Ave., Sausalito, Cal. 94965, is one.

No matter who prepares the introductory comment, it is difficult to walk the narrow line of providing only orientating information without overstepping into preachiness on the one hand or into telling hearers what they ought to think on the other.

If you, the reader, are handed this assignment, here is some help in learning how to do it. Write out what you would say to the congregation in introducing each of the following list of readings. Then check your explanation against the introductory comment of the same number in Appendix A (p. 53).

1. Exodus 34:1–8
2. 2 Samuel 11:26–12:10, 13–15
3. 1 Kings 19:15–16, 19–21
4. Isaiah 40:1–9
5. Matthew 22:1–14
6. Acts 9:26–31
7. 1 Corinthians 15:1–11
8. Galatians 1:11–24
9. Revelation 4:1–11

A word of encouragement: there are no infallibly right words of introduction. What you devise may be better than what I suggest. In any case, be certain that your piece meets the requirements described in the preceding pages and has your minister's approval.

Chapter 8

The Hearing Event

Up to this point we have been thinking about the reader and how he or she can best proclaim God's Word so that members of the congregation may really hear it. Let us now change our focus and consider what is or can be happening to the people to whom the spoken word is addressed.

What happens when you speak to a body of listeners?

We almost never give any thought to this question. Our concern as lay readers is usually all tied up with our doing of it—correct pronunciation, proper volume, timing, poise, and all the rest. What about the listeners? This was our Lord's concern. The Parable of the Sower (Mt. 13:3–9) states that the Word goes forth like seed being planted. Then the parable becomes a description of the hearers—the ground into which the seed falls, concluding with, "He who has ears to hear, let him hear." So let us take a hard look at the recipients of your reading.

The speaker is perceived through the senses—hearing primarily, sight secondarily. Taste, touch, and smell are not involved. We typographic folk, surrounded as we are by the printed word, tend to forget that to oral people— those who do not rely on the printed word—words are heard as having great power. Sound cannot be sounding apart from the use of power.

As a hunter, you can see an elephant, touch, smell, even taste an elephant (if it is dead and you like elephant), but if you *hear* an elephant, look out, something is going on. In this sense all sound, and especially oral utterance which comes from inside a living being, is dynamic. And when we cannot identify a sound, we are likely to assume that it comes from a living being. That is why the psalmist personalizes the sound of an electrical storm:

> The God of glory thunders; . . . .
> The voice of the Lord is a powerful voice. (Ps. 29:3-4)

We do the same thing. If you have ever been lost in the woods at night, every sound is thought to be alive—some threatening animal.

Hearing differs from the other senses. The sound heard communicates with something deep inside the hearer; it goes *into* his consciousness; it reaches HIM. Sight situates the observer outside of what he views, at a distance (it may be a short distance or long), but sound pours into the hearer. Sight comes from one direction; sound can envelop. You can immerse yourself in hearing, in sound. High fidelity is sound at its purest. Walter Ong, a Jesuit scholar in this field, says, "Sight isolates; sound incorporates."[1]

Here is what he means. When a speaker is addressing an audience, the members of the audience normally become a unity, with themselves and with the speaker. A friend tells of having been in the stadium in Nuremberg, Germany, when Hitler addressed the youth rally in 1933. The unity with themselves and with "der Führer" was ominously real.

Speech is by nature social. When you talk out loud to yourself, you are considered some sort of a nut. You

[1] Walter, J. Ong; *Quality and Literacy,* (New York: Methuan Press, 1982), p. 72.

talk out loud to another person. Some observer noticed that sometimes members of a congregation listening to a black preacher, soon and unconsciously start breathing together —"conspiring." Thus the hearers are bound together.

If, however, the speaker asks the audience to read a handout provided for them, as each reader withdraws into his or her own private relationship with the text, the unity of the assembly is fractured. Those around him are less felt, less experienced, less alive. They become background scenery, not persons. Unity is only reestablished when oral speech begins again. "Listening to the spoken word," writes Walter Ong, "turns hearers into a group, a true audience, just as reading a written or printed text turns individuals in on themselves."[2]

In worship our aspiration is, of course, that the assembled people of God become truly an audience so that God's Word may touch their lives. For this bound-together-in-hearing to take place, the people have to listen. The word has to flow over, around, into them. It has to be welcomed, received, absorbed. "Hear that your soul may live," pleads the prophet (Is. 55:3).[3]

When members of the congregation listen to a person as he or she reads Scripture, power emanating from the reader reaches into each of them. They become united;

[2]*Ibid.*, p. 74.
[3]This does not rule out the use of a print-out of the lections in the Sunday bulletin. Some worshipers find that following the reading with the eye is a helpful way of listening. For others, such a practice short circuits true listening. They have found that vocal speech conveys thoughts and feelings not available to vision. Probably the congregation needs some instruction as to the most creative way to use those print-outs in the course of the service. There are also other creative ways of using print-outs of the lections. See Appendix B.

a new bond has been created among them, and with the reader. Something awesome has happened: this moment is for them and for the reader a crucial one. This comes about because the Bible is being experienced in its proper way.

We usually think of the Bible as a printed book. That is not the whole truth. The Bible is primarily a read-aloud-in-public book. That is its natural habitat. The Hebrew word *dabar,* often translated "word," means an event effecting something. It has overtones of force and power. Thus it refers directly to the spoken word. Biblical texts were orally intended—meant to be heard alive, for the spoken word is usually an event, an action in time, something sorely lacking in the thing-like repose of written or printed words. In this connection, it is interesting to note that the strict rule of the Order of St. Benedict instructs monks to read the Bible *with lips* in order to get into it.

Throughout the Bible, God is speaking to his people, not writing to them. As in a play, the Bible is the script. It has an oral mind-set from beginning to end. Consider:

*"In the beginning God *said,* 'Let there be light.' "

*The historical books are stories, told and retold, as is repeatedly evident in the Psalms.

*The books of the prophets are obviously oral passages following, "Thus says the Lord."

*Then in the New Teatement "the Word becomes flesh and dwells among us." The Word-become-flesh is a living presence. God the Father "speaks" himself in his Son; he does not inscribe him. Jesus, the Word of God, left nothing in writing, although we know that he could read and write.

*Even the epistles are sermons intended to be read to congregations.

The matter is summed up by Paul: "The written law kills, but the Spirit [i.e., breath on which rides the spoken word] gives life" (2 Cor. 3:6). Martin Luther knew all this: "That books had to be written . . . is at once a great failure and a weakness of spirit that was enforced by necessity and not by the manner of the New Testament."

Orality, then, is the basic characteristic of the Word of God, the basic characteristic of that Bible which we readers of Scripture inherited from our ancestors in the faith and which it is our privilege and our duty to read to living human beings at worship. And all the characteristics of hearing are raised to a new dimension, because the words the lay readers speaks are the Word of God.

Chapter 9

Upon Hearing the Word of God

The congregation to which you read the Word is composed of a variety of kinds of people. There are the skeptics, the seekers, the waverers, the doubters, and even an agnostic who has accompanied his wife to church. Only the Holy Spirit knows how to reach them all. Your task, as reader, is not to block the Spirit's progress. It may be that the words you read are just what some of those present need to hear and yearn to hear.

Here are some examples:
"Did I not tell you that if you would believe you would see the glory of God?" (Jn. 11:40)

Some hearing doubter sheds his cloak of arrogance, because he is sure the words are addressed to him. Or again:

"Fear not, for I have redeemed you;
I have called you by name, you are mine. . . .
Because you are precious in my eyes,
    and honored, and I love you." (Is. 43:1, 4)

Who knows what secret seeker finds solace in those words or what skeptic reassesses his logical views? Or again:

"I am the Lord, there is no other;
    there is no god beside me,
I will strengthen you though you have not known me."
(NEB, Is. 45:5)

And the agnostic softens his stand and prays the only prayer he can honestly subscribe to, "Lord, I believe, help thou mine unbelief" (Mk. 9:24).

There is also the waverer whose frail faith has been threatened by the trauma of cancer or AIDS, or unemployment or old age. In the company of God's people, she hears,

> "Come to me, all who labor and are heavy laden, and
> I will give you rest." (Mt. 11:28)

She is now able to sing God's praises as she has not done for a long time. Who knows what heavenward gropings are taking place while you are reading God's Word. To the apostle Paul, faith was the deep motivating force in the life of every Christian. So when he writes, "Faith comes by hearing" (Rom. 10:17), he is referring to that kind of profound perceiving. When the hearer feels he has been addressed by the Almighty; he must respond. This is a phenomenon the printed word seldom evokes.

Because hearing the Word has a moving effect, it also awakens a consciousness of mystery, an openness to the infinite, and an appreciation of God's ways in history. It is safe to say that because the hearing of God's Word in worship stirs up a vital faith in those present, it is a significant factor in the ongoing vigorous life of the Christian Church.

Cardinal Martini, the Archbishop of Milan, underscores this significance:

> Beyond question the Church must help the baptized to
> make the transition from a traditional faith based on
> habit and derived from the environment to a personal,

interior faith based on conviction and capable of
resisting the onslaughts of secularism and atheism. This
kind of faith, understood as a dynamic process, is fed
and deepened by hearing the word of God.[1]

There is also a corporate dimension to the effect of
hearing God's Word in worship. As we saw earlier,
hearing has the possibility of binding people together with
their fellow hearers and with the speaker. When that
speaker is only a mouthpiccc for God's Word, a spiritual
dimension of some magnitude has been added.

This became evident during the funeral of Prof.
Thomas Nelson of Virginia Theological Seminary in the
winter of 1940. Dr. Wallace E. Rollins, dean of the
school, read I Corinthians 15:20–58. Later Prof. Albert
T. Mollegen commented on the dean's reading. "Dean
Rollins had not been reading very long before he dropped
out and St. Paul was speaking. But before he finished
Paul dropped out and God was speaking." During his
reading that body of people had become in very truth the
Body of Christ, an entity united with one another and
with God, the Father of all. For God was not only
speaking, he was speaking directly to each hearer present.
Being members of the Body of Christ had become a
reality. So it is that that which we proclaim as a tenet
of faith can become, through the reading of God's Word,
a fact of experience. Thus, as Paul puts it, you make "the
word of God fully known" (Col. 1:25).

We have come a long way in our thinking about the
role of the reader. He/she first must master the mechanics
of the craft, then needs to undergo the discipline of

[1] *Worship*, 61:194 (May 1987).

making the assigned passage intelligible to the hearers. Thus he becomes a responsible participant in the teaching ministry of the Church. Now we see that he/she also has a vital role to play in stirring up a dynamic faith in the hearers and in bringing them to an awareness of being in very truth members of the Body of Christ. Therefore, every lay reader must come to realize that he or she has been assigned an awesomely important part in the gatherings of God's people to worship him.

Chapter 10

Look at the Whole Picture

Lest we lose perspective, let us stand back from our role as readers and look at it in the context of that whole drama, a service of worship.

One's initial awareness is that a church service is a large team operation. It is not a collection of solo performances; it is a group effort. Sometimes we forget how extensive that group is. Look at the list:

—minister or priest in charge of the service

—assisting clergy

—lay readers

—acolytes

—organist

—choir

—altar guild, flower arrangers, metal polishers

—ushers

—sexton

—congregation

—church secretary

—sound engineer

Every church may not have all of these, but every church service involves most of them. Look at the contribution of the team member most likely to be overlooked, the church secretary. Should she happen to mimeograph the church bulletin on the wrong type of paper, the ink smudges. The lady whose white gloves have been soiled with bulletin ink is likely to be so preoccupied during the reading of the Scripture that she does not hear a word of it. So it is that the Sunday service has been sabotaged on the Friday before by an incompetent team member.

Now it is true that reading the Scriptures and the sermon are the most intimately related roles, just as the quarterback and the pass receiver are most intimately related in a football game. But it is because other team members are doing their job properly that the two can function effectively. As Doug Williams, the modest and realistic quarterback of the Washington Redskins, said after they had won the 1988 Superbowl football game, "I didn't do it by myself. . . . If it wasn't for the offensive line, I'd have been mincemeat. Don't just holler 'Doug.' Holler, 'Hogs and receivers.' " In a similar way a church service is a team effort, and the sermon is intended to help worshipers apply to their lives the eternal truths proclaimed in the Scripture readings.

When, however, we seek to fathom the rationale and flow of corporate worship, we discover an even more significant contribution that the reading of Scripture makes. Regardless of denomination, Protestant or Catholic, here is what is taking place in corporate worship. The drama opens with a call to worship, which includes passages of Scripture, a prayer for proper receptivity of that which will follow, some doxological singing. One or more of these create the mood for the hearing of God's Word. As we have seen, that hearing of the Word engenders faith, and this strengthened and deepened conviction of the power and love of God is built upon in the sermon which follows. The preacher is addressing a gathering of faith-filled folk, because of the reading of the Scripture. So it is that their minds are open to receive the Word he will proclaim. Apart from the hearing of Scripture, the sermon would be seed sown on very rocky ground.

In those liturgical churches in which the Lord's Supper becomes the second act of the drama, the reading of Scripture earlier in the service continues to have a significant influence. It is the assembled faith-filled people who gather at the Lord's Table to receive his strengthening gifts. It is undoubtedly their hearing-in-faith earlier in the service which enables worshipers to enter significantly into the climatic moment of the drama around the Lord's Table. Moreover, the awareness of being intimately united with one another, experienced by the hearers during the reading of the Word, now is further enhanced in the breaking of bread together in the Lord's feast. Participants know they are members of the Body of Christ, the family of God.

So the reading of Scripture has laid the foundation for worshipers to enter more deeply into all that comes after. The reader's role in the service is pivotal to the quality and significance of all that follows his/her reading of the Word. Truly, it is no slight thing to be assigned to read God's Word to his people when they come together to worship Him. Accept that responsibility with reverence, and perform it in full awareness of its significance.

This is your commission:

Thus says the Lord God, "Son/[daughter] . . . , go, get you to the house of Israel, and speak with my words to them." (Ezek. 3:4)

Good luck in the Name of the Lord.

Appendix A

Introductory Comments

1. Exodus 34:1-8—When Moses received the Ten Commandments from God on Mt. Sinai, he went down only to find the children of Israel worshiping a golden calf. In his anger, he broke the tablets on which the commandments were written. Now Moses goes up the mountain a second time to receive the commandments from God.

2. 2 Samuel 11:26-12:10, 13-15—Here is a very human story about King David and the wife of Uriah.

3. 1 Kings 19:15-16, 19-21—God tells Elijah the prophet that Elisha is to be his successor. The casting of his mantle on Elisha is the symbolic transfer of authority, and Elisha's farewell meal with his family and friends is a religious celebration.

4. Isaiah 40:1-9—An unknown prophet composed this poem near the end of Israel's Babylonian exile. It foretells the coming of the Messiah and is often thought of in relation to John the Baptist and the coming of Jesus Christ.

5. Matthew 22:1-14—Here are two of Jesus' parables which have been severely allegorized, hence their impossible details. The point of the first is that the Jewish leaders rejected Jesus, so he turned to outcasts and gentiles. In the second, the proper wedding garment represents repentance.

6. Acts 9:26-31—Saul, later known as Paul, had gone

from Jerusalem to Damascus commissioned to arrest any Christians he could find. Enroute he had a vision of the risen Christ and became a Christian himself. Now he returns to Jerusalem, a member of the Church and no longer a persecutor. Here is what happened.

7. 1 Corinthians 15:1-11—This reading is the earliest account of Christ's resurrection appearances, written in 55 A.D., some fifteen years before the first of the four gospels.

8. Galatians 1:11-24—This passage is one of the earliest and perhaps most authentic autobiographical glimpses Paul gives of himself.

9. Revelation 4:1-11—This reading is a sort of prose-poem, in which one feels rather than analyzes the majesty and holiness of God.

Appendix B

Leaflet Print-outs of the Sunday Lections

There are several ways in which churches have made creative use of leaflet print-outs of the Sunday lections.

Some congregations have adult study groups which meet following the service and base their discussions on the Scripture just heard in the service. The print-out leaflets are given out in the group and are a helpful tool in their discussions.

Some other congregations dignify the role of lector by commissioning next Sunday's readers each week at the end of the service. They come forward, are prayed for, and each is presented with a copy of the leaflet print-out of next Sunday's readings.

There are churches which make preparation for next Sunday's service a congregational affair. At the end of the service as the congregation leaves, they are given a copy of next Sunday's lections so that in their private devotions and family prayers they may in concert with the minister or priest be giving prayerful thought to what God's Word will have to say to them the following week.

If the print-out of the lections for the day is to be included in the service leaflet, a major congregational training task has been created. People get a great deal more out of listening to the Word of God, but that is more demanding than following the reading with eyes on a printed page. However, people can be trained to close their eyes and listen, and the benefits are great. They can be trained to use the print-out in the bulletin as a basis for their preservice meditation, or as a focus for one's thoughts while waiting as the other members of the congregation receive communion, or to take home for further meditation on the message of the day. It takes persistent training to get people to use the print-outs in these creative ways. It is, however, well worth the effort.

20, 27, 31, 39, 41